WEDDING ALBUM

Customs and Lore Through the Ages

ALICE LEA MAST TASMAN
Picture Editor: Laurie Platt Winfrey

Walker and Company ✺ *New York*

To my husband, William Tasman
and my children, James Barclay Tasman,
Alice Lea Mast Tasman,
and William Graham Tasman

ACKNOWLEDGMENTS

The author wishes to thank the many individuals and organizations who so kindly cooperated with her in preparing this book, and most especially Mrs. Elsie Sirvatz McGarvey, Curator Emeritus of the Philadelphia Museum of Art and her assistants, Mr. Leroy Bellemey, of the Library of Congress, and John B. Kelly, Jr.

First published in the United States of America in 1982 by the Walker Publishing Company, Inc.

Published simultaneously in Canada by
John Wiley & Sons, Canada Limited, Rexdale, Ontario

Cloth ISBN: 0-8027-0653-3
Paper ISBN: 0-8027-7159-9

Library of Congress Catalog Card Number: 80-50991

Designed by Joyce Cameron Weston
Printed in Hong Kong by South China Printing Company

10 9 8 7 6 5 4 3 2 1

The Aldobrandini Wedding
Detail of Roman fresco in The Vatican

INTRODUCTION

Weddings are, above all, celebrations. In spite of the occasional shot-gun marriage, in spite of marriages of convenience and marriages cold-bloodedly arranged, the enormous majority of weddings are wholeheartedly (if often nervously) celebrated.

Wedding Album is a celebration of weddings —all weddings. After two decades in which unsolemnized cohabitation has gained almost complete acceptance, the United States is seeing more weddings than ever before. And after the barefoot, far-out weddings of the '60s, a surprising number of today's ceremonies are traditional. Brides still wear white, with veils. They are still attended by pastel-clad bridesmaids; the formally dressed groom is still buttressed by his best man and a flock of ushers.

Even if some of the old practices are gone, the spirit is the same. Although it is more common than it used to be for a couple to finance their own nuptials—or at least contribute to them— most Fathers of the Bride still find themselves facing a depleted checking account with mixed feelings. Although the newlyweds may have

been living together for a year or several, the old honeymoon jokes are still circulating.

Weddings have been celebrations, all through the ages. Customs and superstitions have arisen thick and various around the act of getting married. Young people embarking on what is one of the most sudden and severe rites of passage in every culture can reassure themselves with rituals hallowed by time and generations.

Weddings are celebrations everywhere. Some —in the Orient, in Scandinavia—last for days. (Some in the United States last for days, too; extended and bibulous wedding celebrations did not completely go out with Scott Fitzgerald.)

And weddings are celebrations for the tradespeople who make their living from them. Jewelers offer advice along with diamond engagement rings, wedding bands and assorted accessory items. Florists devise ever more elaborate (and expensive) bouquets and decorations. Bakers outdo one another in the grandeur of their wedding cakes. Couturiers and just plain clothing manufacturers feature the wedding gown as the climax of their fashion shows.

"Bridal consultants" have their own trade association. A whole industry has arisen to "package" a wedding for the far-from-well-to-do. For a set and reasonable fee, a couple can contract for just about everything but the bride's dress: men's clothing (to rent), food, table settings, invitations, flowers, photographer, limousine, favors—the works. One New York City firm, Receptions Plus, handles over a thousand such events a year. Weddings are definitely *not* out of date!

The magic is still there, and for everyone—old and young, rich and poor, celebrity and next-door neighbor, peasant and sophisticate. It is potent magic; evidence on every hand attests to that.

Share the magic. Join us at the wedding celebrations in this album. Have a wonderful time!

It starts with a proposal, even though today's suitor is unlikely to be on bended knee, as is the petitioner for the young woman's hand in this 1903 stereopticon slide (left).

(opposite) In the 1920s, Evelyn Waugh, recorder of the doings of the "bright young things" of England's moneyed classes, epitomized the desire to shock the bourgeoisie when he had two of his characters hold their wedding in a captive dirigible. Starting in the 1960s, many young couples chose to leave the formality of church or hotel ballroom and marry under the skies, in costumes that were more colorful than conventional, not because they were out to shock but to make their nuptial ceremonies more an occasion uniquely their own.

(overleaf) The professional wedding photographer and his camera were still in the future in 1805. The nuptials of this demure American bride and her tailcoated groom were nevertheless captured for posterity in pen and watercolor by an unknown artist—possibly one of the itinerant painters of the period.

A MARRIAGE HAS BEEN ARRANGED

"Of all actions of a man's life, his marriage does least concern other people; yet of all actions of our life, 'tis most meddled with by other people."

John Selden, *Table-Talk*

All over the world, pairing of man and woman in matrimony has been, and in many countries still is, a profession. (Where it is that no longer, it remains a fascinating hobby for busybodies.)

The adventurers who journeyed to California in the nineteenth century found opportunity, beautiful growing weather and sometimes gold. Although women of easy virtue were usually on hand, potential wives were in lamentably short supply. Ingenious entrepreneurs rushed to fill the need, as this French cartoon of the period humorously comments *(right)*. "Marriage Enterprises has an assortment of widows to reclaim the most miserable household," the sign advises. Below it, the industrious matrimonial agent packs a profitable shipment for the Western frontier.

In Turkey, a more traditional type of matchmaker looks over a crop of "possibles," in order to be able to offer the freshest items to her clients *(opposite, top)*.

Arranged marriages were once the custom in our own society, and certainly were common among the native Americans who preceded the European settlers. Although the details in this French engraving of an American Indian marriage proposal *(left)* may be somewhat fanciful, the custom, which included the offering of a token gift, did exist. In our own culture, the practice survives in our vocabulary, if nowhere else—"asking for the young woman's hand," "giving the bride away," are common examples.

In parts of China, as elsewhere, parents still arrange marriages, and the bride and groom may never meet until almost time for the wedding. But traditional Chinese ritual offered prenuptial ceremonies that gave the young couple a chance to see what they were soon to be getting *(opposite, center and bottom)*.

"Nobody ever works as hard for his money as the man who marries it."

Frank Hubbard

An arranged marriage is a business proposition, and like any other is accompanied by an exchange of wealth. The groom might buy a wife by paying her family a brideprice; and in some Oriental and African societies, a man had better have both boy and girl children so that the large sums his sons must pay for their wives can be balanced by those they receive for their daughters. In one region of India, parents of daughters who have no chance at a wealthy bridegroom save face by first "marrying" a girl to a bunch of flowers, which are then thrown down a well. Now she is a "widow," and her parents can accept a nominal brideprice for her without shame.

A dowry—wealth that the bride brings to her groom—is a more widespread form of marriage payment. It may be material goods or less tangible assets: a rise in social class, for example, or the business advantage of a merger of families. What, then, is to be done when the bride's family has no assets?

Young women without dowries provided an opportunity for the charitable in times past. St. Nicholas, the prototype of Santa Claus, furnished dowries from his considerable fortune for all three daughters of an impoverished nobleman. And in eighteenth-century France, an unknown benefactor donated the dowries for "ten poor girls," who lost no time in taking advantage of the bounty (*below*).

Wedding gifts are a somewhat disguised form of dowry, in which friends and relatives take on some of the burden. Few offerings, however, could match the variety and extent of this array (*opposite*) garnered by Queen Victoria when she married her Albert and displayed to the public at Britain's Marlborough House.

WEDDING GOODS

Russia may have undergone two revolutions in this century and countless other political changes, but the samovar is still as indispensable an adjunct to the Russian home as it was in Tolstoy's time—and long before. The gleaming tea machine *(opposite, above)* is the core of a Soviet bride's trousseau.

This German bride proudly counts the *pfennigs* saved up for six years to buy her wedding clothes *(below)*. If she conforms strictly to custom, she will spend her pennies on her bridal shoes.

The famous Tiffany diamond engagement ring *(opposite, below)*, created in the 1870s and an American tradition for over a century.

At a wedding in the State of Israel, the presiding rabbi reads from the *Ketuba,* the Jewish marriage contract *(top)*. The *Ketuba* is an important part of the Orthodox Jewish marriage, and in Israel, as in the United States, there are illuminators who make the documents into works of art that not only set forth all the agreements of property and conduct between bride and groom but are objects of beauty and sentiment to be treasured and passed down to children and grandchildren.

The *Ketuba* by the New York artist Betsy Teutsch *(below, left)*, the one by calligrapher M. Rosenstein of Philadelphia *(below, center)*, and the heading of an ancient *Ketuba* from eighteenth-century Venice showing a view of Jerusalem *(below, right)* give some notion of the range of styles and illustrations these marriage contracts encompass.

MATRIMONIAL LAW

"Nil metuit licito fusa puella toro." ("The girl who lies on a lawful bed knows no fear.")
Petronius, *Fragments*

Adam and Eve were married only in the sight of God, but as soon as individuals became part of a larger society, the State stepped in and soon there were volumes of laws dealing with matrimony.

One such law in nineteenth-century England absolved married women of their debts and made their husbands responsible. Seizing on the opportunity of solving her financial problems, a woman of fashion who had lost everything at the gaming tables would hasten to Newgate prison on the morning of an execution, bringing a clergyman along. There she would be married to the condemned criminal just before he was hanged, with her I.O.U.s on his soul, if not his conscience.

In today's United States, couples must still deal with the State, paying their few dollars for the license that records their union in the official rolls. Here Norman Rockwell takes a characteristically sentimental look at young love on the way to the altar in his painting for *The Saturday Evening Post*, "The Marriage License".

The cartoonist C.F. Budd had a somewhat more satiric notion of marriage preliminaries in this drawing *(below)* from a 1911 *Life,* the old humor magazine that bore that name before Henry Luce bought the title for his glossy picture periodical.

But whether the arrangements were legal or merely familial, bargaining difficulties could arise, and sometimes the haggling would continue even while the wedding party waited nervously on the sidelines, as in the German engraving of 1896 *(opposite)* .

R.Grieß.

TO DRESS THE BRIDE

"A woman seldom asks advice before she has bought her wedding clothes."
Joseph Addison, in *The Spectator*

The wedding dresses on the opposite page were part of an exhibition, "The Bride in Fashion," held some years ago at the Philadelphia Museum of Art. Donated by Philadelphia residents and restored by the museum staff and by students, the thirty dresses in the exhibit covered 140 years, from 1798 to 1958. They reveal a surprising variety of different styles in the bridal gowns American women have worn since their country was new.

Although most of the dresses are white, the one in the top row at left is of purple taffeta, a choice of color made to signify mourning for the bride's father, killed in battle during the then-recent Civil War.

The origin in the Western world of the custom that links orange blossoms to weddings is sometimes traced to the Crusaders, who are believed to have brought it back from the Saracens. Others claim the Moors introduced it when they overran Spain. Few modern brides are aware of its symbolism and do not know that when they carry or wear the white blossoms they are demonstrating a desire for fecundity. The orange blossoms that trim the center gown in the top row are artificial, and an old superstition is that these must be burned within a month of the wedding or bad luck will follow.

In the latter nineteenth and early twentieth centuries, the fashion was to pile on ornamentation, and designers seemed to vie with one another in decking their wedding gowns with as much fringe, braid, pleated ruffling, shirring, lace and other embellishments as the yardage could encompass. The ivory-figured-silk with a lace veil *(top row, right)* is simple compared to the shirred and embroidered confection next to it *(second row, left)*, or the looped, fringed, pleat-trimmed gray taffeta *(second row, center)*. The passion for decoration reaches a peak in the dress in the second row at right. Of gold-figured-silk, it is trimmed with white fringed satin and gold-covered balls, and has white shirred satin with gold folds at the front of the skirt. The train has a wide white satin pleat trimmed with white fringed satin ruffling and bows and lace edging.

The earliest costume in the Philadelphia exhibit is, appropriately, a Quaker wedding gown of tan taffeta with a matching bonnet and simple white shawl *(third row, left)*.

An Empire dress from the turn of the nineteenth century, white satin with a floral stripe *(third row, second from left)*, and a very simple and beautiful white embroidered cotton gown *(third row, second from right)*.

Although its lines are simple, the beige satin fabric figured with green and gold leaves gives this mid-nineteenth-century wedding dress its air of quiet elegance and distinction *(third row, right)*.

From the 1870s to the end of the century, wedding gowns took on a tailored look. The four in the fourth row could all have been based on conventional woman's suit patterns, although their gala purpose dictated trimming that transformed them to something much more festive—particularly the bedizened dress on the right.

Relatively modern wedding dresses *(bottom, first three from left)* concentrate on line rather than decoration and are thus simpler than most of those that came before them, although the classic gown at the far right could be worn by today's formal bride without alteration—provided she has a 22-inch waist!

1865

1879

1847

1902

1877

1879

1798

1800

1830

1840

1875

1880

1880

1895

1941

1952

1958

1865

"There is something about a wedding-gown
Prettier than any other gown in the world."
    Douglas Jerrold, *Douglas Jerrold's Wit*

Until about two hundred years ago, there was no such thing as "a wedding gown". To be sure, the bride wanted to look her most beautiful on this special day, and to that end usually acquired a new dress for the ceremony. But it was no more a wedding gown than any other "best" dress she might have chosen for a different special occasion.

Nor was it necessarily white. Although Anne of Brittany was the first noted bride in modern history to wear all white at her wedding in 1498 to Louis XII of France, brides continued to walk to the altar in almost any color that became them best, and until quite recently, a young Icelandic woman's dream was to have a black velvet wedding dress embroidered in silver and gold. (Green, however, was taboo everywhere but in Norway, being either an unlucky color reserved for the fairies, the color of jealousy or a symbol of grass stains that hinted of illicit romps in the meadow.)

Church aisles must have been wider in the eighteenth century; otherwise, how would the bride in pale blue *(left)* have made her way to the altar?

In 1834, hoops were more moderate, but the shoulders of this Paris bridal costume vied with them *(right)*. (It is interesting to speculate on the engineering difficulties involved in attaching the veil securely to the extension on the model's elaborate coiffure.)

Godey's Lady's Book was the fashion periodical of its day. The issue of December, 1862, shows a raft of Civil War era brides *(opposite, above)* —and two well-behaved flower girls.

This bride's attendant, as well as the bride herself, reflects the style of 1903: tight skirt, exaggerated bosom, tiny waist and leg-o'-mutton sleeves *(opposite, left)*.

"The dawn of a beautiful day," is the caption on the drawing of a rapturous bride of the early 1920s *(opposite, right)* —although her lap dog looks as though he has his own disruptive plans. As in the 1903 drawing, the bridal dress here reflects the transitory fashion of the period to a greater degree than many of our traditional wedding gowns today.

L'autre est la fleurette rustique
Eclose au pays des meuniers
C'est la fleur austère et pudique
Qui fleurit deux fois nos landiers.
BOTREL.

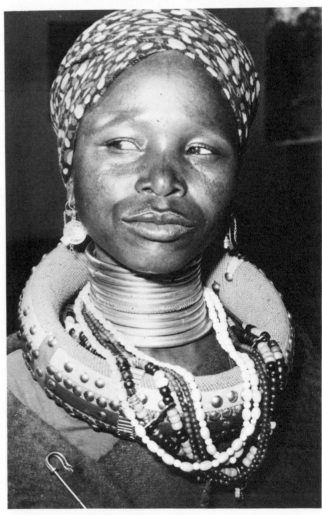

More than white satin and lace can go to dress a bride. The desire to look particularly beautiful on the wedding day is worldwide—and takes various forms.

A bridal party from the Sfax district of Tunisia (*opposite, above*) . The bride's care-fully-worked veil and elaborate jewelry seem, at the moment, to be eclipsed by her obviously new and very businesslike wristwatch.

This proud Ndebele (South Africa) bride dis-plays the jewelry she has fashioned herself to wear at her wedding (*opposite, right*) .

From France's Pont–Aven (*opposite, left*) a young woman wearing a wedding dress embroi-dered by hand and faithful to the style worn in this part of Brittany for centuries.

The winsome bride (*below*) from Soviet Russia has made a gala version of the region's traditional headdress—a wedding confection of pearls and fanciful flowers.

On the first and second nights of a Malay wedding, which goes on for several days, the bride sits in state with her groom, leaving periodically to change her costume (*left*). She may display as many as twenty different ones—some from her trousseau, others provided by the *mak andam*, an essential character in these affairs. The *mak andam* dresses the bride's hair, makes her up, lends her genuine jewelry, furnishes a bedspread for the nuptial bed and the dais on which the couple sits. She also provides moral support and helps with the numerous costume changes.

At a Hindu wedding, brides wear ornate saris and as much jewelry as they can find (*opposite, left*). Some of it is the groom's engagement present to them, some is their own, and those who cannot afford as lavish a display as they would like rent additional ornaments.

This bride in Sri Lanka (formerly Ceylon) wears a silk sari worked with gold (*right*). The gold and diamond ornaments on her head symbolize the sun and moon, and the pendant earrings are an obligatory part of her costume. For the ceremony, she will don ten necklaces—seven pendants set with rubies, pearls and diamonds; a long chain of beads formed to look like various fruits; a chain of linked gold pieces in the shape of flower petals; and a *pol mal male*, an ornate chain inspired by the coconut flower.

The ornate headdress of the cheerful Hungarian bride in native costume (*opposite, right*) is her own handiwork, made especially for her wedding.

Yellow roses and baby's breath add a distinctive look to the conventional veil of this U.S. bride (*opposite, below*).

Rich or poor, or somewhere in between, the bride planning a formal wedding is ready to spend not only money but time and thought in choosing the dress of her dreams. She scans fashion magazines, visualizing herself in the perfect bridal gown—as the perfect bride.

Then, in department store or bridal shop, or at the family sewing machine, she must translate the dream into reality—often being forced to scale it down a bit in the process.

The bride with money to spare might buy an exclusive design, or have one made expressly for her.

At the other end of the scale are shops like Madame Campanella's Bridal Aisle on New York's busy Fourteenth Street. Madame's prices are within reach of the impecunious young working women who patronize her store and other Fourteenth-Street bridal shops. Although many of them are in an advanced state of pregnancy, it does not deter them from their desire for a formal wedding gown with veil and all the proper accessories—to be ready in one or two weeks.

(*opposite*) Bridal costume for a forgotten 1934 moving picture.

(*below, top*) The cover of *Vogue* magazine's bridal issue of April, 1940.

(*below, bottom*) A 1942 department store bridal window.

This modern bride wears a dress designed and made especially for her—by her mother (*opposite*).

If the bride-to-be is a film star or a president's daughter, she can realize her dream by selecting a wedding gown from the top of Priscilla of Boston's collection. The nation's leading designer of bridal clothes has sold more than forty of a recent $3,000 model. But her large collection also contains more basic styles, at somewhat lower prices, although, as she says, "Today's bride saves her own money—and spends it."

Priscilla of Boston's pearl-embroidered lace wedding dress (*top*), crown of her collection for spring and summer of 1980.

Each of the thousands of pearls that outline the Alençon lace motifs on the Priscilla gown is sewn on by hand in the designer's workrooms (*bottom*).

... AND THE GROOM

"A man looks pretty small at a wedding, George. All those good women standing shoulder to shoulder, making sure the knot's tied in a mighty public way."

Thornton Wilder, *Our Town*

Although the bride is the visual center of attention, the groom has not always been content to fade into the background in a uniform of morning coat and top hat. In the mid-nineteenth century, a man of consequence may have worn a conventional black suit, but he dressed it up with accessories like the cream-colored figured-silk stock collar under a variously flowered waistcoat, and carried a lace-edged hand-

kerchief *(left)*. For out-of-doors, the dandy donned a feather-bedecked soft hat.

Later (1889) the white waistcoat, high silk hat, white gloves and cane marked a man of fashion on his way to the altar *(right)*.

Hungarian Count Szechenyi *(opposite, left)* chose this elegant uniform, with fur cape, jeweled chain and even a sword, for his marriage to heiress Gladys Vanderbilt in 1907.

An Oriental groom's costume *(opposite, right)* is at least as ornate as his bride's, as this young man of Singapore demonstrates.

When the German ski racer Luggi Leitner married Renate Fritz (in an appropriate snow shower) he, as well as his bride, wore the traditional clothes of the region *(opposite, below)*.

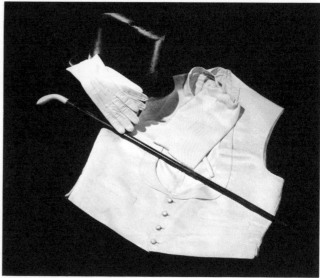

Wedding Day
was there in his
marriage finery,
a little the worse
for wear.

PRELIMINARY PARTIES

"I gravely doubt whether women were ever married by capture. I think they pretended to be—as they still do." G.K. Chesterton

The modern bride's attendants and her groom's best man and ushers are survivals from more robust times, when it was expected of a man that he acquire his wife by capturing her. She surrounded herself with her female friends, whose duty it was to keep her from being carried away. The groom, therefore, enlisted his male companions to help him steal his intended from her home.

Deadly serious at first, bride stealing eventually turned into an enjoyable ritual. The suspense went out of it, but the horseplay of what had become a game entertained all the participants.

Originally, the "bride's maids" wore clothes exactly like those of the bride herself in order to confuse the marauding young men. To this day, at formal weddings, the bridesmaids dress alike (their gowns are sometimes of different colors but the same design), although they no longer echo the bride herself.

The friends who reinforced the battling bride and groom were rewarded with tokens—ribbons and such—which later became objects of more worth and from which the custom of giving gifts to the wedding party derives.

A merry bridesmaids' dinner in New York City in 1905 (*below*).

German brides-to-be following their country's old custom have a different kind of fun; while the groom and his comrades are enjoying a bibulous stag night, the bride and her friends hold a *Polterabend* in front of her house. They smash cups and dishes—all the available crockery— against the front door, and the bride then must sweep up all the debris. The noise of crashing crockery is said to frighten away evil spirits, and the sweeping-up operation brings luck to the newly wedded couple throughout their married life.

(*opposite*) One of the famous series by illustrator Walter Crane in 1901. His personification of "Wedding Day" seems jaunty enough in spite of a bachelor bash the night before.

GETTING THERE

"The music at a wedding procession always reminds me of the music of soldiers going into battle."
Heinrich Heine

In other cultures, and in our own past, an important part of the marriage celebration has been the wedding procession. On foot, on horseback, in carriages or motor cars, the party proceeds to the place for the ceremony in an atmosphere of mingled display, gaiety and ancient superstition.

In England, horses and carriages for this journey ideally were gray—a lucky color—and traditional couples still demand gray for the color of the automobiles that have replaced them. In Normandy, the horses' harnesses were scarlet, the prescribed hue for frightening away witches.

Often musicians led the procession, and formerly the bridesmaids and flower girls carried sheaves of wheat—natural or gilded—a sign of fertility. By sympathetic magic, where to suggest a desired result is to create it, the men of the party bore symbols of wealth, their value depending on the economic status of the participants.

Village Britons had a more practical way of gathering "wealth"—household objects and furniture; they proceeded to the wedding in a cart called a "bridewain," stopping at each household on the way and garnering gifts to start them on their married life. It was the early equivalent of today's bridal shower.

(*opposite*) Amid a flash of fireworks and astride a dappled mare, Shah Jahan rides to the lavish wedding celebration of his favorite son, Dara Shokoh. To his left is the veiled bridegroom. Jahan is best known in the Western world as the monarch who built the magnificent Taj Mahal in memory of the most beloved of his wives, Mumtaz.

(*below*) Fiddlers lead this early nineteenth-century Austrian wedding procession. The miniature adults directly behind them are the artist's misrepresentation of the children of the party; the couple following them are the bride and groom.

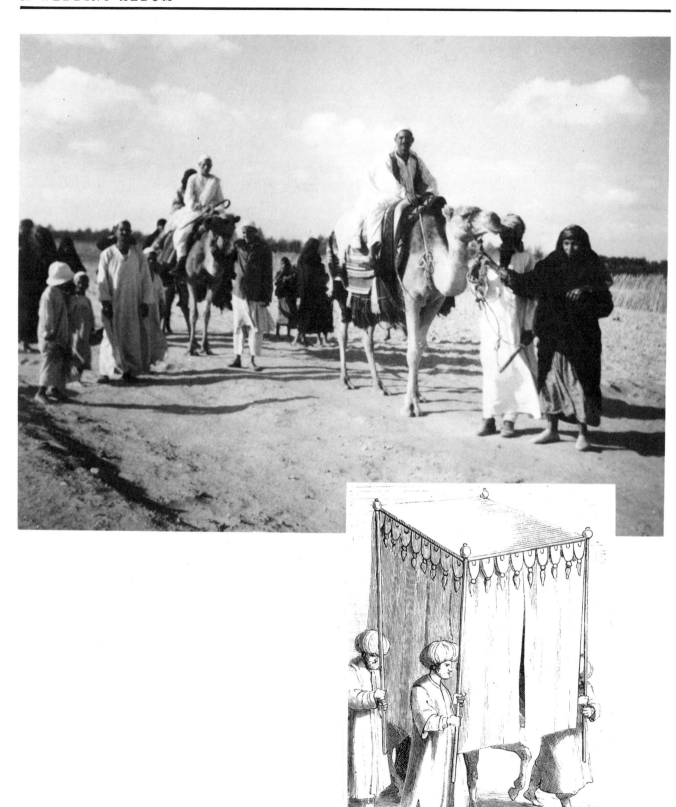

In contrast to the display of most wedding processions, certain cultures demand that the bride be hidden on the way to her marriage. Ancient Chinese enclosed her in a windowless sedan chair; in traditional Turkish practice, the bride rode on a horse, but four men walked along beside it carrying a curtained canopy (*opposite, below*).

The Arabic bride rode to her wedding behind her father on the omnipresent camel, her groom preceding her, as he would continue to do in every aspect of her married life (*opposite, above*).

This detailed—and labeled—engraving (*top*) shows the wedding procession of Frederick V, "The Winter King" of Bohemia, who in 1613 married Princess Elizabeth of England, daughter of James I. Through their daughter, Sophia, mother of England's George I, they founded the House of Hanover from which the present English royal family is descended.

A less elaborate, but very fashionable, German wedding of the present day (*bottom*). Coach, coachman's livery and horses are white, the color of good fortune for marriages in that country.

THE CEREMONY

"The voice that breathed o'er Eden
That earliest wedding-day
The primal marriage blessing,
It hath not passed away."

John Keble, *Holy Matrimony*

The universal significance that attaches to weddings is reflected in their popularity as a subject for artists.

In 1434, Jan van Eyck painted one Giovanni Arnolfini and his bride, Giovanna Cenami, and the double portrait (*opposite*) has become one of the best-known and most-often-reproduced wedding paintings in the world.

(*below*) The subject of the marriage ceremony and its attendant celebrations was a popular theme of the eighteenth-century English artist William Hogarth. His "The Wedding of Stephen Beckingham and Mary Cox" has symbolic cupids showering the nuptial pair with flowers from a golden cornucopia.

Now, as at this wedding in 1880 *(opposite)*, a Russian Orthodox ceremony demands that both bride and groom stand under crowns held by attendants. Here the priest is offering the bride a sip of the ceremonial wine. Bride and groom drink three times from the same cup of wine, symbolizing their willingness to sample the same cup of experience.

A solemn ceremony, indeed, judging by the grave expressions of the participants in this medieval wedding *(right)*.

Centuries later, in the America of 1902, a wedding is still a grave affair for some, as the stereopticon slide illustrates *(left)*.

N. Currier, of Currier and Ives, designed the 1948 marriage certificate below, which not only attests to a legal union but presents a picture of an idealized ceremony and quotations from Scriptures regarding the duties of Husband and Wife.

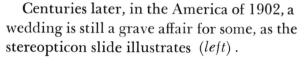

In the Christian world there was a time when the wedding ceremony was not a religious one, even among devout churchgoers. But it was thought to be lucky to be married at the door of the church, and, in time, the wedding moved into the building and under the wing of the clergy.

In other societies marriages are generally, but not exclusively, associated with the predominant religion. Whether religious or not, however, the wedding is an important rite of passage in almost every culture and is celebrated with intricate and often splendid ritual.

A Hindu wedding, like these in India, is unrivaled for the color of its trappings: the bride's jewels, the gorgeous saris of the female guests,

the flowers that decorate the chamber—and the groom.

A priest performs the special religious rites exclusive to the groom as the bride looks on (*opposite, above*). When these preliminaries are over, she will be brought into the proceedings.

The wedding couple in front of the holy fire that symbolizes the eternal flame of love, surrounded by trays containing offerings of fruits and flowers (*opposite, below*).

Bride and groom exchange garlands of flowers (*left*). Note the groom's elaborate headdress of the same blossoms.

Close friends play their part in the ceremony of a Hindu wedding (*right*).

A marriage in Thailand (*below*) is performed either by the parent of the bride or groom or by a very highly respected friend of one or both families. The ceremony is held in the bride's home, in the presence of family and attendants.

The couple is blessed and given a talk about proper conduct as a married pair. The rope around their heads, called a "brahman rope," is the symbolic tie that binds them together and is supposed to bring them happiness and luck.

A Malaysian marriage ceremony: the entire wedding party is in Islamic dress (*opposite, top*).

A wedding in the Gulf province of Papua New Guinea, where the ancient native customs still are very much alive (*opposite, center*).

(*opposite, bottom*) Detail from a series of paintings of a Chinese wedding. As the bride and groom bow to heaven, a boy sets off celebratory fireworks in back of the altar.

"I saw all Israel scattered upon the hills . . ."
Old Testament, First Book of Kings

The Jewish people, dispersed throughout the world for centuries, have carried their religion and their customs to every corner of the earth, in every era since the destruction of the Temple. Although Jewish weddings, like the Jews themselves, have adapted to the culture and the period in which they occur, they retain a unique identification through all their metamorphoses.

Rembrandt's psychologically penetrating "The Jewish Bride" (*opposite*) was a creation of the master Dutch painter's later life and re-flects his vision of what set his people apart from other Dutch burghers.

The French artist Delacroix was intrigued by the exotic. "Wedding Scene in Morocco," with its African background and Jewish participants, was doubly fascinating to him (*left*).

In today's New York City, a wedding of Orthodox Jews follows tradition, as evidenced by the behatted groom and totally veiled bride (*right*). The *chupah,* or canopy, beneath which the couple stands is used even in the most modern, country-club Jewish ceremonies, where it is often an expensive tapestry woven of fresh flowers.

"Marriage is popular because it combines the maximum of temptation with the maximum of opportunity."

George Bernard Shaw

Seven hundred and ninety Korean and foreign couples, all members of Rev. Sun Myung Moon's "Holy Spirit Association for the Unification of World Christianity," were married at this mass wedding in downtown Seoul, Korea. The wedding guests numbered some eight thousand, a figure that a bride could toss at her parents when they complain about the length of her guest list.

*"And what have kings that privates have not too,
    Save ceremony . . ."*
    William Shakespeare, *Henry V*, Act IV

Royal weddings are by definition affairs of grandeur and glittering trappings, and the art that immortalizes them captures their excitement. Here three royal Marys are shown at their marriage ceremonies:

Peter Paul Rubens painted the wedding of France's Henry IV to Marie de' Medici in 1600 at the church of Santa Maria del Fiore in Florence (*left*).

Charles Le Brun, the chief designer of the Gobelins tapestry works in seventeenth-century France, created a great series of fourteen tapestries commemorating the achievements of Louis XIV. This one (*right*) shows his wedding to the Spanish princess Marie Thérèse in 1660.

(*opposite*) In 1810 Napoleon, crowned Emperor of France, had his marriage to Josephine annulled because she could not bear him children, and married Marie Louise, daughter of Emperor Francis I of Austria. The French artist G. Rouget set down the royal event for posterity.

An anonymous engraver left the world a wedding portrait of the Duke of Burgundy with his bride *(inset)*, who became his duchess in 1697.

In modern times and far-off lands: The Emperor Hirohito of Japan and his Empress at their wedding ceremony in 1959 *(below)*. The ceremonial robes they wear are identical to those worn by Japanese royalty a thousand years before.

New York socialite Hope Cooke married Maharajkumar Thondup Namgyal, the then-crown prince of the Himalayan kingdom of Sikkim, in a Buddhist ceremony *(opposite)*. The bridegroom, in a yellow brocaded silk jacket and orange silk gown, sits on a three-foot throne, with his bride on a slightly lower platform.

Of all the royal houses in the Western world, the British is the best-known and still the most glamourous. The present monarch's great-great-grandmama, Queen Victoria, married her cousin, Prince Albert of Saxe-Coburg-Gotha, in 1840 in Westminster Abbey *(left)* .

Queen Elizabeth II, Crown Princess at the time of her marriage in 1947, and her groom, Philip Mountbatten, Duke of Edinburgh *(right)*.

(opposite) The present Queen's daughter, Princess Anne, and her groom, British army officer Mark Phillips, after their marriage in 1973.

ROYAL MOTHER, ROYAL DAUGHTER

Her Serene Highness, Princess Grace of Monaco (*opposite*), at the time of her marriage to Rainier, reigning prince of that tiny Riviera principality. The former film star Grace Kelly wears a gown created for her by the Hollywood designer Helen Rose, whose original sketch (*inset*) better illustrates the intricate detail that went into it.

Princess Caroline, (*below*) daughter of Princess Grace and Prince Rainier, wears orange blossoms in her hair for her wedding to Phillipe Junot.

FEASTS AND FROLICS

*"The guests are met
The feast is set . . ."*

Samuel Taylor Coleridge,
The Ancient Mariner

Whether among sixteenth-century Flemish peasants, eighteenth-century upper-class Britons —indeed, among almost any peoples of the world, the celebration of a marriage involves feasting and frolicking.

"Peasant Wedding" (*below*), painted around 1566 by Pieter Breughel the Elder, captures the merriment of villagers in his native Flanders.

Marriage à la Mode, a series of illustrations showing the profligate and pointless existence of a fashionable young English couple, is considered to be the masterpiece of satirical artist William Hogarth. This scene (*opposite*) from the series depicts "The Wedding Dance" and dates from 1745.

A joyful newly married Cape Malay couple, the groom in Islamic dress, hurries down the aisle after their ceremony (*left*).

At a fashionable wedding in South Africa, guests throw serpentine rather than rice at the pair emerging from the church (*opposite, top left*).

This Norwegian bride and groom (*right*) go at top speed to their night-long celebration, in a horse-drawn carriage. The fiddler is continually present at the five-day observance in the farm community of Voss, a village in the mountains of Norway's fjord country famous for keeping alive the old wedding traditions of the area.

The village loans the crown the young woman wears to all its brides. About two hundred guests will consume a barrel of *akavit* and four or five barrels of beer; the *kuogmester,* or master of ceremonies, will contribute song after song; and one of the features of the festivities will be the "long dance," when the fiddler and the bridal couple lead the guests from one farm to another all day, with a drink at every stop and continuous fiddling and dancing.

(*opposite, top right*) In Papua New Guinea, drummers provide the music for a native wedding celebration.

Indian newlyweds, with a young relative, sit at the head of the wedding table wearing ropes of flowers (*opposite, center left*).

Starched white traditional headdresses predominate in the scene (*opposite, center right*) of an outdoor marriage feast in Brittany.

A Kandyan bridegroom in Sri Lanka (Ceylon) feeds his bride with milk rice cake, which signifies good fortune at all auspicious and ceremonial occasions in that country (*opposite, bottom*).

2952. Noce Bretonne

RECORDING THE EVENT

*"Let all thy joys be as the month of May
And all thy days be as a marriage day."*
Francis Quarles, *To a Bride*

Happy brides and bridegrooms cherish the memory of their wedding day, but they want a more tangible record, as well. This was as true in the sixteenth century, when Lorenzo Lotto painted his "Bridal Couple: Messer Marsilio and His Wife" (*below*), as it is today, when the charming young Cuban bride and groom opposite posed for an informal wedding picture outside the church where they were married.

Brides and grooms, wedding parties, from different times and different places, all very aware of the camera and of the importance of the day.

A double wedding portrait in the nineteenth century: The Breton brides *(left)*, clearly sisters and possibly twins, wear traditional finery, the mustachioed grooms dress alike in brass-buttoned uniforms.

Lou Beager and his bride pose self-consciously in a Nebraska field on their wedding day in 1889 for a lovely bit of Americana *(right)*.

(opposite, above) Albany, Minnesota in 1912; the epitome of a small-town wedding scene.

The delightful wedding party picture *(opposite, below)* says "1920s" as plainly as though it were embroidered on the maid of honor's satin hat brim.

(overleaf) The Peruvian wedding party had a unique background for their photo memento half a century or more ago: the oldest church in Ayacucho, built shortly after the town was founded by Francisco Pizarro in 1539.

Oriental newlyweds sit—or stand—for their wedding portraits: The elaborate and beautiful traditional dress of the Japanese bride (*opposite*) contrasts with her groom's sober Western attire.

Below, a wedding party in Singapore solemnly faces the camera.

CAKES AND FLOWERS

"I sing of brooks, of blossoms, birds, and bowers:
Of April, May, of June, and July flowers.
I sing of Maypoles, Hock-carts, wassails, wakes,
Of bridegrooms, brides, and of their bridal
*   cakes."*   Robert Herrick, *Hesperides*

The Romans gave us wedding cakes; theirs were made of water, barley, flour and salt. Until relatively recently, weddings boasted two cakes: one light, iced in white, and eaten at the wedding feast, represented the bride; the other, the groom's cake, was a dark, rich fruit cake, to be cut into small pieces and put away for anniver- saries and distributed to the guests. At some modern weddings, the custom survives: the bottom layers of a cake are white—the "lady's cake"—while the upper sections are of fruit cake, to be stored for later celebrations.

Famous cakes for famous weddings: The magnificent edifice on the right was created for the wedding of Victoria, Princess Royal of England, Queen Victoria's daughter, and Prince Frederick William of Prussia, later Frederick III, in 1858.

Below, Senator John F. Kennedy and his bride, the former Jacqueline Bouvier, cut the cake at their wedding. (Left is brother Robert Kennedy.)

"What woman, however old, has not the bridal-favours and raiment stowed away, and packed in lavender, in the inmost cupboards of her heart?"

William Makepeace Thackeray,
The Virginians

The bride's bouquet, too, can be said to stem from the Romans. It was their custom to light the first fire in a couple's new house with a torch, which was then tossed out to be caught by one of the wedding party. The practical French, in the fourteenth century, substituted the harmless bouquet for the torch and started the superstition that whoever among the bride's attendants caught the blossoms would be the next to marry.

The new Mrs. Kennedy tosses her bridal bouquet from a staircase as she goes up to change into her traveling clothes.

When President Grover Cleveland and his former ward, Frances Folsom, were married in 1886, the table centerpiece (*bottom*) was this rather extraordinary floral creation.

HYMEN

UNINVITED GUESTS

"For next to that interesting job
The hanging of Jack, or Bill, or Bob,
There's nothing so draws a London mob
As the noosing of very rich people."

Thomas Hood,
Miss Kilmansegg, Her Courtship

To the rich and famous, the photographer is not always a welcome member of the wedding, and often strenuous efforts are made to exclude the people with the cameras and their pencil-and-notebook colleagues.

Below, David Eisenhower and his bride, the former Julie Nixon, seem happy enough to be accosted by the news hawks, but the earlier-day *paparazzi* (*opposite, top*) obviously have been waiting a long time to snap the picture of some V.I.P.

Longer ago, in 1908, society reporters (*opposite, below*) at the wedding of Gladys Vanderbilt and Count Szechenyi had to peer through the fence in the January cold for a glimpse of the couple they were assigned to cover.

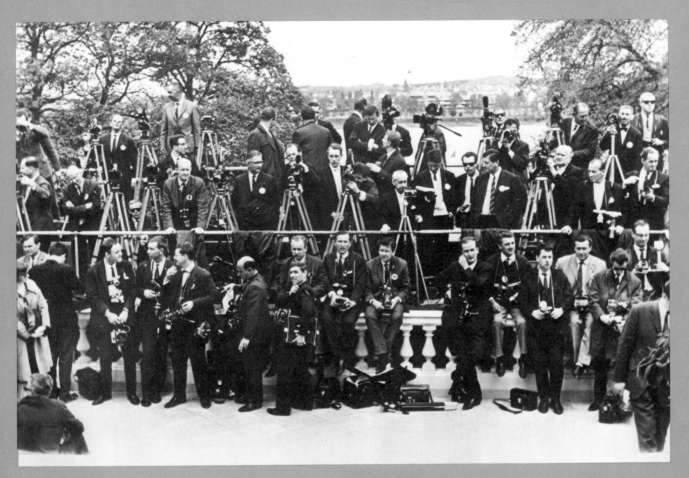

WHITE HOUSE WEDDINGS

A marriage ceremony in the Executive Mansion always commands the attention of the entire nation. There have been several such occasions, but only once was the president himself the groom, when Cleveland married the beautiful Miss Folsom (*opposite, left*).

President "Teddy" Roosevelt was a flamboyant personality, but his daughter Alice, as she subsequently demonstrated, had the quick wit and sharp tongue to capture continuous public attention in her own right. Here, she and her groom, Nicholas Longworth, at her right, pose with the President at Alice's wedding in 1906 (*opposite, right*).

(*opposite, below*) Jessie, daughter of the World War I president, Woodrow Wilson, surrounded by her bridesmaids, each clutching an enormous beribboned bouquet.

The wedding party of Lynda Bird Johnson and Charles Robb in 1967 (*left*) when the bride's father, Lyndon Johnson, was president. The group is photographed in a room of the Executive Mansion under a portrait of The Father of His Country.

Tricia, daughter of Richard Nixon, married Edward Cox in the White House garden (*right*) during her father's abruptly ended incumbency.

MARRIAGE AT THE MOVIES

"It's an experiment frequently tried."
W.S. Gilbert

Film stars have the reputation—with some exceptions an earned one—of marrying often. The roles they play also call for frequent marriages, before the camera. These wedding scenes are from three early motion pictures, two of them indisputably classics, the third certainly a box office smash in its time.

Below, Marlene Dietrich in one of her most famous roles, the husky-voiced singer in *The Blue Angel,* with her doting schoolmaster groom, played by Emil Jannings (1930).

Chanteur Maurice Chevalier and songbird Jeanette MacDonald seem too wrapped up in one another to notice the priest waiting to marry them in the wedding scene from their 1929 early "talkie," *The Love Parade (opposite, above)*.

Claudette Colbert on the arm of Walter Connolly playing her father as they film the elaborate society wedding for the 1934 comedy hit, *It Happened One Night.* Ms. Colbert's eventual groom in the picture, '30s superstar Clark Gable, is missing from this shot *(opposite, below)*.

Sometimes the obligatory "boy-gets-girl" ending of the Hollywood movie required strong measures on the part of the scriptwriters:

In *The Graduate* (1967) *(left)* Dustin Hoffman, undaunted by having arrived at the church just after the ceremony, makes off with Katharine Ross—who really wanted to marry him anyhow instead of her hapless groom.

Thanks, perhaps, to his horse Tony, silent cowboy star Tom Mix is able to abduct *his* leading lady before the marriage is final, carrying her away under the startled eyes of an obviously fashionable wedding party *(right)*. The scene is from the silent movie, *Lucky Horseshoe*.

And sometimes, in the movies, boy *never* gets girl, or vice versa. Waiting at the church are a puzzled Edward G. Robinson in *Silver Dollar* (1932) and a despondent Anne Nagel in *A Bride for Henry* (1937).

(*opposite, above*) Leslie Howard as Ashley Wilkes, Vivien Leigh as the bride (Scarlett O'Hara, of course) and Olivia De Havilland as Melanie in that monument of Hollywood films, *Gone With the Wind* (1959).

The Philadelphia Story (1940) (*left*) and its musical version, *High Society*. In the first, Jimmy Stewart and Ruth Hussey, as the newspaper team, flank the bride and her second-time-around groom, Katharine Hepburn and Cary Grant, with John Halliday (at Ms. Hussey's

right) as the father of the bride. In the musical (1956), an earnest Bing Crosby and a radiant Grace Kelly stand before the minister, with Sidney Blackmer in the Halliday role. Frank Sinatra played the newspaperman in this version, Celeste Holm his reporter girlfriend.

A formal wedding couple larger than life in their informal setting: Katharine Hepburn and Spencer Tracy leave their runaway wedding ceremony in *Woman of the Year* (1942) (*opposite, below*).

Jean-Paul Belmondo and Catherine Deneuve are wed in a 1970 French film improbably titled *Mississippi Mermaid* (*right*) .

French star Jeanne Moreau as the not-very-grieving widow in *The Bride Wore Black* (1968) (*left*).

Cinema celebrations: *Godfather* Marlon Brando honors the bride with a wedding dance in the 1972 blockbuster about The Family (*opposite, above*) .

The marriage of Steven (John Savage, fourth from left) and Angela (Rutanya Alda, at his left) in *The Deer Hunter* (1978) . Other celebrants are, from left, John Cazale as Stan, Chuck Aspegren as Axel, Robert De Niro as Michael, Christopher Walken as Nick and Meryl Streep as Linda (*opposite, below*).

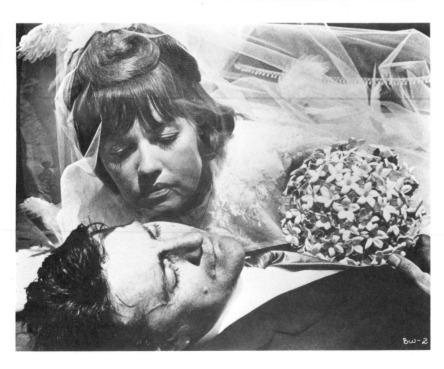

THE MUCH-MARRIED

"Marriage is hardly a thing one can do now and then—except in America." Oscar Wilde

Film star Elizabeth Taylor has been kept busy with weddings both on screen and off.

With Spencer Tracy in *Father of the Bride* (*opposite, top left*).

Six husbands, seven weddings (*below*). The husbands: Top row, Conrad Hilton, Jr.; Michael Wilding; Mike Todd, whose marriage to Ms. Taylor ended when he died in a plane crash. Bottom row, Eddie Fisher; Richard Burton (two takes on that one); present husband John Warner.

In 1959, Taylor and husband #4, singer Eddie Fisher (*opposite, top right*), leave the county courthouse in Las Vegas, Nevada, where Fisher netted two birds with one stone, obtaining both his divorce from actress Debbie Reynolds and his license to marry Ms. Taylor. A few hours later, they put the document to use in a Las Vegas synagogue.

Taylor and Burton at their second wedding in the exotic grounds of Chobe Game Park in Botswana, Africa. Officiating is the Botswana marriage officer Ambrose Masalila (*opposite, below right*).

The seventh splicing, another *alfresco* affair: Ms. Taylor and Warner (*opposite, below left*).

SENSATIONS

"I have found it impossible to carry the heavy burden of responsibility and to discharge my duties as King as I would wish to do without the help and support of the woman I love."

King Edward VIII, farewell broadcast

(*opposite*) Edward VIII became merely Duke of Windsor when he abdicated the British throne in 1936 in order to be free to marry the American divorcée, Wallis Warfield Simpson.

The affair was a scandal of international proportions—and it enthralled the gossip-loving public.

Jacqueline Bouvier married Senator John F. Kennedy in 1953, and to the public they were the epitome of glamour—the "Camelot Couple" (*left*). In 1968, by then a president's widow, Mrs. Kennedy made a second marriage that was fabulous in a quite different way—to Greek multi-multi-millionaire Aristotle Onassis, many years her senior (*right*) . The gossips had a field day.

MAY . . .

Political considerations sometimes accounted for extremely early marriages in royal families. Below, Louis, titular Duke of Burgundy and grandson of Louis XIV, was fifteen when he married Marie Adelaide, Princess of Savoy, and his little bride was even younger. Louis became heir to the throne when his father, the Grand Dauphin, died before Louis XIV, but he, too, did not live to be king; the couple's son eventually inherited the crown as Louis XV.

The large gentleman second from right in the foreground is the Sun King himself; on his left stands the groom's father, the Dauphin. The marriage is being celebrated by a Cardinal, and the King's morganatic wife, Mme. de Maintenon, appears between Louis XIV and the Dauphin. The clothes and the portraits, the un-

known artist assures us, were "drawn from Life," as was the setting, the chapel at Versailles.

The enchanting child opposite is a Tamil from Sri Lanka (Ceylon) —and poses on her wedding day at the alarming age of eight!

. . . AND SEPTEMBER—
OR POSSIBLY EVEN LATER

A few years ago, in Grassau, Germany, one-hundred-year-old Robert Koch led seventy-seven-year-old Magdalena Klein to the altar (*opposite, below*). It was not the first marriage for either, and the festive table, piled high with roast meat and dumplings, could hardly accommodate all the children, grandchildren, and great-grandchildren brought together by this union.

MILITARY WEDDINGS

The grooms are variously uniformed, but the bride of a military man can be beautiful in a wedding gown.

The early nineteenth-century genre painter Richard Caton Woodville captured the simple happiness of "The Sailor's Wedding" in his native Baltimore in this charming painting (*below*).

More than a century later, during World War II, another U.S. sailor (*opposite, left*) takes a bride.

Just after World War I, a Miss Rolland of the American Red Cross Auto Service and a Captain Delehanty of the 308th Infantry were married at a military wedding in France (*opposite, right*), and all the customs were observed. Rifles for the arch were certainly plentiful, but finding the bride's and bridesmaids' dresses may have taken some doing in the war-torn country.

Unholy joy: The happy bride and bridegroom (*opposite, below*) are Nazidom's second-in-command, Air Marshal General Herman Goering and his new wife, Emmy. The general wears one of the elaborate bemedalled uniforms in which he loved to swathe his portly frame.

Behind the bridegroom, and obviously the guest who must have outshone even the principals at this 1936 occasion in Berlin, is *Der Führer* himself. An entire Nazi division seems to be assembled on the steps behind the newlyweds.

AND NOW FOR SOMETHING COMPLETELY DIFFERENT ...

*"If you wish women to love you, be original.
I knew a man who wore felt boots in summer
and winter, and women fell in love with him."*
Anton Chekhov

For some couples, the most elaborate formal
wedding is too tame. So they seek inspiration in
their hobbies, their jobs, or their lifestyles to
find a unique setting for the tying of their nuptial knot. Or else they just look around for the
most out-of-the-ordinary location they can find
to stage one of the world's most common events.

The "I do" would come out as an unintelli-
gible gurgle at the wedding (*left*) in an aquar-
ium at Sea World in Orlando, Florida. So the
bride and groom, diving enthusiasts both, carry
signs to signify their intention of loving, honor-
ing and cherishing as they take the plunge into
matrimony.

A marriage that already has its ups and downs
(*right*). The ceremony was performed on the
Revolution roller coaster in Valencia, California's Magic Mountain amusement park.

Neither swords nor rifles, but hockey sticks
and flower-ornamented wire brushes (for sweep-
ing out chimneys) form the arches under which
these happy couples leave the altar (*opposite,
top and center*). Gliding into married life is
Greg Post, a member of the Shamrocks, San
Francisco's hockey team, and his bride, Sandra
Fonteno. The spotless (on this day, at least)
new husband and wife are master chimney
sweeps David Stoll and Dee Miller. Colleagues
from all around the country, in traditional
working clothes, came to their wedding on the
103rd floor of Chicago's Sears Tower.

The bride wore—well, a white veil, anyhow,
if nothing else. The groom wore nothing at all—
the presiding justice of the peace was the only
one with special permission to appear clothed at
this nudist wedding in (unsurprisingly) Las
Vegas.

"The winds have welcomed you with softness"
—from the balloon prayer

Bridal balloons are nothing new, as this early twentieth-century photograph shows. The bride and groom arranged to be wed just before embarking on the National Balloon Race in Kansas City, Missouri.

(*opposite*) A lighter-than-air wedding still has charms for some. In Frederick, Colorado, an hour-long flight gave Diane Baumbach and Jerry Weiman time for their ceremony and a soar over the green countryside before touching down to celebrate with guests on the ground.

PICTURE CREDITS

Air-India Library: *p. 25 top left; pp. 42-43 all* □ **Associated Press:** *p. 72; p. 85 right, both* □ **Bettman Archive:** *p. 8 left; p. 10; pp. 40-41 all; p. 47 bottom; p. 54 right; p. 65 top; pp. 66-67; p. 70 top; p. 86; p. 89 top; p. 94* □ **Bibliotèque Nationale, Paris:** *p. 52 top; p. 88* □ **Brown Brothers:** *p. 36 top; p. 91 top, both* □ **Ceylon Tourist Board, New York:** *p. 24 right; p. 61 bottom* □ **Courtesy Condé Nast:** *p. 27 top* □ **Consulate-General of Israel:** *p. 14 top* □ **German Information Center:** *p. 12; p. 31 bottom; p. 37 bottom; p. 89 bottom* □ **Courtesy of H.S.H. Princess Grace of Monaco and Mr. Jack Kelly (Howell Conant):** *p. 56 full page; p. 57* □ **IBUSZ Hungarian Travel Bureau:** *p. 25 top right* □ **Japan Tourist Bureau (Nihon Hasshoku):** *p. 68* □ **Jewish National and University Library, Jerusalem:** *p. 14 bottom right* □ **Kunsthistorisches Museum, Vienna:** *p. 58* □ **Library of Congress:** *p. 27 bottom; p. 31 top left; p. 71 bottom; p. 73 bottom; p. 74 all; p. 75 top; p. 91 bottom* □ **Library of Congress/courtesy Magnum:** *p. 71 top; p. 87 left* □ **London Telegraph (Woodfin Camp):** *p. 55* □ **Louvre:** *p. 47 top; p. 51 left* □ **Courtesy June Massell:** *p. 62* □ **Metropolitan Museum of Art, Marquand Fund, 1936:** *p. 38* □ **Mobilier National, Paris (Giraudon):** *p. 51 right* □ **Musée des Arts et Traditions Populaires, Paris:** *p. 22 bottom left; p. 61 center right; p. 64 left* □ **Museum of Modern Art Film Stills Archive:** *pp. 76, 77, 78, 80, 81, 82, 83 all; p. 85 top left* □ **Museum of the City of New York, Byron Collection:** *p. 33* □ **National Archives, White House Photo Collection:** *p. 75 bottom* □ **National Gallery, London, Reproduced by courtesy of the Trustees:** *p. 39* □ **National Museum, Delhi:** *p. 35* □ **Nebraska State Historical Society, Solomon D. Butcher Collection:** *p. 64, right* □ **New York Public Library, Picture Collection:** *p. 8 right; p. 9 all; p. 11; p. 17; pp. 20-21 all; p. 26; p. 32; p. 34; p. 36 bottom; p. 37 top; p. 45 bottom; p. 54 left; p. 70 bottom; p. 79 both; p. 96* □ **Norwegian Travel Office, New York:** *p. 60 right* □ **Old Corner House, Stockbridge, Mass.:** *p. 15* □ **Papua New Guinea Office of Information:** *p. 45 center; p. 61 top right*

□ **Philadelphia Museum of Art:** *pp. 6-7,* The Edgar William and Bernice Chrysler Garbisch Collection; *p. 19 top row (#1)* given by Mrs. Laussat R. Rogers, *(#2 & #3)* given by Bertha Lippincott Coles; *p. 19 second row (#1)* given by Mrs. Raymond John Girvin, *(#2)* given by Mr. and Mrs. Samuel Wanamaker Fales, *(#3)* given by Mrs. James Mapes Dodge; *p. 19 third row (#1)* given by Mrs. Percival Parrish, *(#2)* given by Mrs. Paul Reid Tait, *(#3)* given by Mrs. Theodore Heysham, Jr., *(#4)* given by Mr. Henry G. Beerits; *p. 19 fourth row (#1)* given by Mrs. Lionel Levy, *(#2)* given by Mrs. W. Hobart Porter, *(#3)* given by Miss Josephine F. Howell, *(#4)* given by Mrs. Jay Besson Rudolphy; *p. 19 fifth row (#1)* given by Mrs. Henry Lyne, *(#2)* given by Mrs. Jay Besson Rudolphy, *(#3)* given by Mrs. Stephen I. Bookbinder, *(#4)* given by Mr. Arthur Williams *(all* photographed by the Philadelphia Museum of Art); *p. 30 left* given by Mrs. Sarah A. Roberts; *right* given anonymously; *p. 56 inset* given by Her Serene Highness, the Princess Grace of Monaco (A. J. Wyatt) □ **Photo Researchers (Suzanne Szasz):** *p. 5* □ **Photos by Anthony:** *p. 28* □ **Prado:** *p. 63* □ **Priscilla of Boston (Betsy Kidder):** *p. 29 both* □ **Receptions Plus:** *p. 25 bottom* □ **Rijksmuseum, Amsterdam:** *p. 46* □ **Henry T. Rockwell:** *p. 16* □ **Courtesy of M. Rosenstein:** *p. 14 bottom center* □ **Singapore Tourist Promotion Board:** *p. 24 left; p. 31 top right; p. 69* □ **South African Consulate-General, New York:** *p. 22 bottom right; p. 45 top; p. 60 left; p. 61 top left* □ **Soviet Consulate-General (Fotokhronika, Tass):** *p. 13 top; p. 23* □ **Barry Staver:** *p. 95* □ **Courtesy of Mrs. William Tasman:** *p. 65 bottom,* author's parents' wedding □ **Tate Gallery, London:** *p. 59* □ **Courtesy of Betsy Teutsch:** *p. 14 bottom left* □ **Tourist Organization of Thailand:** *p. 44* □ **Tiffany & Co.:** *p. 13 bottom* □ **Tunisian National Tourist Office:** *p. 22 top* □ **U.P.I.:** *pp. 48-49; p. 92 left; p. 93 bottom* □ **Vatican Library, Rome (Giraudon):** *p. 3* □ **Versailles (Lauros-Giraudon):** *p. 50* □ **Walters Art Gallery, Baltimore:** *p. 90* □ **Wide World Photos:** *p. 53; p. 73 top; p. 84; p. 92 right; p. 93 top and center* □ **Courtesy of Carey Winfrey:** *p. 61 center left* □ **Courtesy of Laurie Platt Winfrey:** *p. 4*